The Self-P
Checklist

How to Prepare Your Manuscript for
Print-on-Demand Publishing and
Promote Your Book

The Self-Publishing Checklist

How to Prepare Your Manuscript for
Print-on-Demand Publishing and
Promote Your Book

Andy Baldwin

www.bookstandpublishing.com

Published by
Bookstand Publishing
Morgan Hill, CA 95037
1594_32

ISBN 1-58909-063-2

Printed in the United States of America

**Print-on-Demand Publishing
Since 1996**

Are You Ready to Publish Your Book?
Make it Happen!

Contact Us Today — We Can Help!

1-866-793-9365

❧ **Preface** ❧

Welcome to Self-Publishing

Welcome to the world of Self-Publishing! Congratulations on taking the next step in your writing career! At Bookstand Publishing, we help authors publish their works as perfect-bound trade paperback, full-color trade paperback, and case-bound hardcover printed books.

Regardless of whom you choose to do the final printing of your book, *The Self-Publishing Checklist* will answer many of your questions about print-on-demand publishing, and give you basic, acceptable formatting instructions applicable to any reputable print-on-demand publisher.

By utilizing Bookstand Publishing, you maintain full control over your work. No long-term contracts are involved. We are book printers, e-commerce providers, and eBook experts. You retain your rights, all of them. Our agreement is very clear.

This book is an example comprising the exact quality of paper, printed text, and cover stock that Bookstand Publishing uses to print both black-and-white and full-color paperback books. Your book will match the same high quality and appearance of this book.

Our hardcover titles feature typical case binding, with gold foil lettering on the spines, full-color dust jackets, and ivory paper.

Bookstand Publishing is a tool for you to use to gain access to and exposure with more readers. We give you the ability to produce and distribute your work as a "bookstore-quality" "trade paperback" or "case-bound" book and retain more of the profits. We even offer a wholesale ordering system to cost-effectively offer short runs of your book.

Bookstand Publishing lists all of our books on Amazon.com and BarnesandNoble.com. Your book will also be available through Ingram, the largest book wholesaler in the United States. This means that your book will be available to the largest book markets throughout the United States and abroad.

We also offer a variety of editing and marketing services to help ensure your book is successful.

If you would like to discuss your publishing project, please give us a call at 1-866-793-9365 or email us at support@bookstandpublishing.com

Andy Baldwin
Bookstand Publishing
Print-on-Demand Publishing Services
305 Vineyard Town Center, Suite 302
Morgan Hill, CA 95037
Telephone (866) 793-9365
Internet: http://www.bookstandpublishing.com
E-mail: andy@bookstandpublishing.com

Here Is What Bookstand Publishing Can Do For You

Bookstand Publishing offers authors a global marketplace for their books.

Our Packages Offer These Features:
Books Published in 6 to 8 Weeks
Full-Color Cover or Dust Jacket
- (Cover Design — Additional Fee)

Unlimited Photos, Tables, and Charts
ISBN Registration Number
Bar Code
Books In Print Registration
e-Commerce Web Page for Your Book
Electronic Proof
Printed Proof
Author Retains ALL Rights
PDF eBook Available for Sale
Wholesale Purchase Program
Online Promotional Information
Distribution through our Ingram channels, including:
- Amazon.com
- BarnesandNoble.com

30% Royalty on Books sold from your e-Commerce page
50% Royalty on e-Books sold from your e-Commerce page
10% Royalty on sales through other retail channels

Trade Paperback (Perfect-Bound)
Black-and-White Interior
48 Copies of Your Book

Hardcover (Case-Bound with Dust Jacket)
Black-and-White Interior
10 Copies of Your Book

Full-Color Trade Paperback (Perfect-Bound)
Full-Color Interior
48 Copies of Your Book

Marketing

e-Commerce Web Page

Distribution on <u>Amazon.com</u> and <u>BarneandNoble.com</u>

Distribution through Ingram and Baker & Taylor

Wholesale Purchase Program

Press Release Preparation

Press Release Distribution

Sell Sheets

Full-Color Postcards

Full-Color Bookmarks

Full-Color Book Signing Posters

Through <u>www.WebHostingForAuthors.com</u> we also offer:

- Book Website Domain Names
- Website Tonight (Click and build your own website online)
- Custom Book Website Development
- Book Website Hosting

Table of Contents

Appendix

Writing a book is an adventure. To begin with, it is a toy and an amusement. Then it becomes a mistress, then it becomes a master, then it becomes a tyrant. The last phase is that just as you are about to be reconciled to your servitude, you kill the monster and fling him to the public.

– Winston Churchill

❧ **1** ❧

Is Self-Publishing for You?

When considering whether or not to self-publish your book, keep in mind that traditional publishers publish much less than 1% of all unsolicited manuscripts they receive each year. Many industry insiders estimate the amount to be 0.1%. If you fall into the 99.9% that they reject, you will probably be very frustrated with that process, but you won't be alone.

With self-publishing, you take control of your own destiny. Make your book a success yourself!

Ten years ago, if you could not interest a traditional publisher in your book, you could spend tens of thousands of dollars preparing your book and thousands of dollars more with a custom printer to fill your garage with boxes of books. Thanks to digital printing technology, however, it is now possible to obtain a professional quality copy of your book for under $1,500. With Bookstand Publishing, you receive 48 copies of your book in the initial printing. The initial printing is included in the publishing package price. Visit our web site at www.bookstandpublishing.com for a list of all the benefits of publishing with Bookstand Publishing.

Here are a few questions you may want to ask yourself:

1. What is your motivation and purpose for publishing your book?

Writing a book is a lot of work. Publishing one is even more work. Is your purpose clear and sufficiently well conceived to sustain you through the experience? If profit is a motive, then the venture must be treated as a business. Typically, from start to finish, a writer will spend 10% of his or her time writing the book, 15% publishing it, and 75% marketing and promoting the finished book. Keep your purpose clear!

2. Is your book written for a specific market niche or group of people?

It is more expensive to promote a book to a wide general audience. Marketing costs are less when the target audience is specific, definable, and accessible.

3. Do you have a way to sell books direct?

Selling books direct (at retail price to your target audience) is the most profitable way to recover your initial self-publishing investment. The standard heavy discounts to wholesalers and bookstores can be costly for slow-moving books. In fact, without a solid marketing plan, selling books to bookstores can be the least profitable way to distribute your book. Think of alternative ways to distribute your book: Organizations, associations, corporations, conventions, fundraisers, and back-of-the-room sales after lectures or workshops, to name but a few. These are known as special sales markets.

4. Are you willing to go out and promote your book?

A general rule for authors: A book stops selling when the author does. No matter who publishes your book, you are responsible for creating the demand for it. A book will not sell well sitting on a bookstore's shelf, unless interest is generated for your book. Don't forget: Writing a book is about 10% of the effort, publishing it is about 15%, and marketing it is 75%!

5. How many copies do you think you will sell?

Beyond your friends and family, who will be interested in your book? Knowing your market and how to reach those people are important questions to answer before you invest in self-publishing. The fact is that 95% of all books published sell fewer than 7,500 copies. With Bookstand Publishing's print-on-demand services, though, you will not incur the added expense of printing thousands of copies of your book, only to stockpile them in your garage.

6. What is Print-on-Demand (POD)?

At its simplest, print-on-demand (POD) publishing means that whenever a book is demanded (ordered, bought, requested), a copy of the book is printed to fill that specific demand.

Self -Publishing Fact:

Feed Me, I'm Yours by Vicky Lansky sold 300,000 copies before she sold the book to Bantam, which sold 8 million more.

Self-Publishing Facts:

Tim O'Reilly, President of O'Reilly & Associates, started out as a self-publisher of books on UNIX. He now runs the fourth largest trade computer book publisher, which grew out of his self-publishing efforts.

❧ **2** ❧

What Are the Costs Involved?

How Much Does it Cost and How Much Can I Make Per Book Sold?

The publishing package costs vary with the trim size of the book and the number of pages. Bookstand Publishing offers books in five trim sizes (all are listed in inches):

- 5.25 x 8.25
- 5.5 x 8.50
- 6 x 9
- 7 x 10
- 8.5 x 11

The most popular and economical trim size is 5.25 x 8.25. Your book can be bound on either edge, so your book can be in either portrait or landscape format. For up-to-date pricing information, please visit the following:

Trade Paperback:
www.bookstandpublishing.com/content/paperbackservices

Case-Bound with a Dust Jacket:
www.bookstandpublishing.com/content/hard_cover_services

Full-Color Paperback:
www.bookstandpublishing.com/content/full_color_books

Cover Art Options:
Bookstand Publishing offers you four options for your book's cover art.

1. Author-supplied artwork
   a. You are welcome to supply a cover art file matching our specifications for free. Once received, we will have one of our graphics professionals review the file prior to printing.
2. Available template cover designs
   a. Multiple designs to choose from
      i. Theme cover designs
      ii. Deluxe cover designs
      iii. Basic cover designs
   b. View examples of our template cover designs at: www.bookstandpublishing.com/content/cover_art
3. Insert a photograph or image on one of our cover templates
   a. A photo can be inserted onto any one of our cover templates for only $25.
   b. The photo must be in a TIFF or JPEG format and be at least 300 dpi.
   c. You can find some great cover photos at www.istock.com or other stock photo website.
4. Custom-designed by our graphics professionals. We can take your cover idea and create a print-ready, high-resolution cover art file. You own all the rights to this file upon its completion.

For current pricing, please visit:
www.bookstandpublishing.com/graphic_services.php

Whether you choose one of our cover art templates or have us custom-design a cover for you, all of our cover art is created by graphic design professionals.

If you choose paperback, you will receive 48 copies of your book as perfect-bound bookstore-quality paperbacks with full-color laminated 80-pound covers. If you choose case-bound hardcover, you will receive 10 copies of your book unless you order more at the time of printing. The full-color paperback packages include 48 copies as well.

You will receive an International Standard Book Number (ISBN) for your printed book, and your book will be listed in Bowker's *Books In Print*.

You will receive your own web page and have your book offered for sale in its paperback form, as well as in eBook form in PDF file format. The eBook will not have a unique ISBN, but will use the printed version's ISBN.

We create the credit card processing mechanism to process the orders and ship the books to the customers.

Royalties are paid monthly if they total or exceed $25.00. If royalties in a given month are below $25.00, then they will be allowed to accumulate, and will be paid once they total or exceed $25.00. Royalty amounts vary based on the type of book binding and the sales channels. Please refer to our website for complete details.

You will always have the option to purchase additional books at competitive wholesale prices if you choose to sell books on your own. Our wholesale order system is available for a minimum order of 25 copies.

Self-Publishing Facts:

Irish-born British playwright and author George Bernard Shaw started out as a jobbing printer who self-published some of his own work. He went on to write many famous plays, including *Pygmalion* and *Saint Joan*. In addition, he founded the Fabian Society and won the 1925 Nobel Prize for Literature.

Below are a few samples of our available cover art templates:

Sample Deluxe Cover Templates

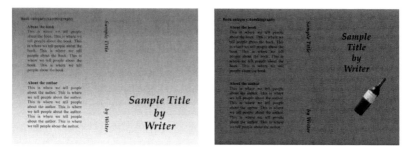

Sample Basic Cover Templates
(These templates can be customized by adding a photo
or changing the background color)

Each cover design will have a fully qualified EAN bar code on the back
cover along with the category classification, summary, and, if space
permits, the author's biography. The bar code will contain the ISBN and
price in U.S. dollars.

The cover samples above are only a few of the templates offered by
Bookstand Publishing. You can view all of the examples in color, and in
larger size, at:
www.bookstandpublishing.com/content/cover_art

ജ **3** ഃ

Wholesale Ordering

Unique to the industry, Bookstand Publishing provides a password-protected wholesale ordering system for its authors. This provides you with the ability to cost-effectively purchase small quantities of your book at any time.

This service is integral to your success, as you should have a few copies of your book on hand at all times. Additionally, you can sell your book in catalogs, from your own web page, at seminars, in local bookstores, etc. By using our wholesale ordering system, you can purchase your book at a deep discount and make more money from each sale.

The average wholesale cost of each book is 30% of the retail price, or *up to 70% off the retail price*! The minimum purchase quantity is 25. Shipping is extra. Wholesale orders typically arrive about two weeks after the order is placed.

Self-Publishing Facts:

Novelist Nathaniel Hawthorne, author of *The House of the Seven Gables*, *The Scarlet Letter*, and other American classics, paid for the publication of his first book.

✥ 4 ✥

Important Basic Formatting Rules

<u>Let's Get Your Book Ready!</u>

The following suggestions will help you format your book file for professional-looking consistency in its appearance and feel.

Always use your TAB and/or ALIGNMENT TOOLS to move and align text. Using spaces to position text can result in inconsistent spacing, particularly when different fonts and typeface sizes are used in the text.

Always use the PAGE BREAK function to advance to the next needed page if the text itself does not flow to the next page.

The overuse of the spacebar and/or carriage return is more work and will cause problems in the future with formatting.

NEVER in the creation of your book use the ENTER key at a line's end to force a return. Let the software do its job.

Always save changes as you go.

The use of long document names also causes problems. Use "book_1," then "book_2," etc., for each revised version of your file as you proceed.

PLEASE do not label the book with long extraneous titles such as, "My book. About dogs and cats/1st edition 7/23/2001.doc."

If you have questions or need help, please ask before you get started.

Self-Publishing Facts:

Scott Adams, creator of the *Dilbert* comic strip and book series, self-published an original eBook, *God's Debris*, early in 2001 as a way of testing the market for a new book. As a result, he was able to get an "unusually good deal" from his regular publisher, Andrews McMeel, when he sold them the book rights.

∞ **5** ∞

The Submission Checklist

Use this checklist as you create your manuscript file.

- ❑   The book is in a word processing file.
- ❑   The book is ONE file.
- ❑   The book is done in *Microsoft Word*. If the book is in any other software program it can be converted, but please contact us BEFORE you proceed.
- ❑   The book is set in single pages, not columns or two-page layouts, and the page size is set to the finished size.
- ❑   The cover artwork is separate from the book file.
- ❑   The cover artwork is a TIFF or JPEG file and a minimum of 300 dpi.

This is everything we require.

When your book is ready you can email to us at andy@bookstandpublishing.com and we can give you a quote or you can submit your file online at www.bookstandpublishing.com by choosing the package of your choice and uploading your manuscript during the registration process.

Deepak Chopra vanity-published his first book and then sold the rights to Crown Publishing. The book became the first of many best sellers for him.

ॐ **6** ॲ

The Formatting Checklist

If you wish, you can format your book yourself. This is NOT required, but many authors prefer to format their books themselves so they can be sure their books looks exactly like they want.

Use the checklist in this chapter to format your book yourself.

❑ Be sure your book is in ONE electronic file.
❑ Review the Template near the end of this book.
❑ **Set up your page size**. (The following example is in *Microsoft Word 97-2003*. Other programs may be similar.)
❑ The most common and most economical of our trim sizes is 5.25 inches wide x 8.25 inches tall. To format to our other sizes, please change the "PAPER SIZE" per the following instructions. All other adjustments stay the same.

❑ **In *MICROSOFT WORD*, open a NEW Document and go to PAGE SETUP.**

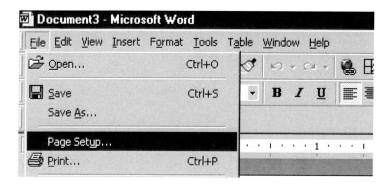

❑   **Set your PAPER SIZE to Custom 5.25" x 8.25".**

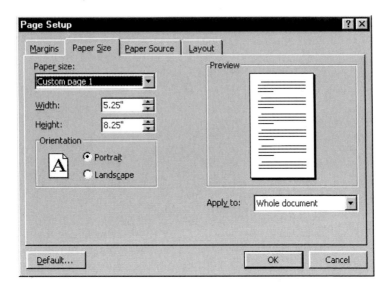

❑ **Set your MARGINS to the following:**

❑ **Format your PARAGRAPHS** to FULL Justified and Single Spaced. Indent the first sentence of the paragraph using the SPECIAL box and FIRST LINE by 0.5" as shown below. No spaces between paragraphs.

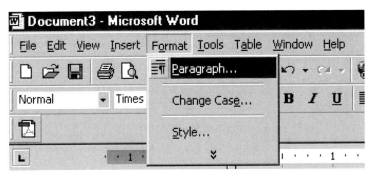

❏   **You are now ready to put your book into this format**. Close your existing book file. With the above described blank document open in *Microsoft Word*, go to the top Tool Bar; to the right of FILE, EDIT, and VIEW, you will see INSERT. Click INSERT, then FILE. The window that should contain your existing book file will then open. Select your book and click INSERT. You have now put your book in the correct basic format.

For word processing programs other than *Microsoft Word*, please consult your program's HELP feature to determine how to achieve the same results. If your book is in separate files, for example each chapter in its own file, you must INSERT Chapter One, then place the cursor at the END of Chapter One and INSERT Chapter Two, and so on, into the main book file.

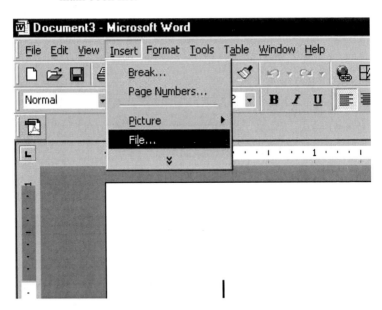

❏   Once the file has been inserted, view the page size on your screen at 75% or as TWO PAGES. This will make the chapter location and the page numbering easier to visualize.

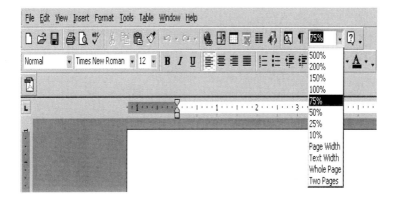

❑ **Body Text** should be set to 10 point Times New Roman text font. Actually, you may use any font you want; however, it is best to use an easy-to-read font. Also, keep the font and the font size consistent for a professional-looking book.

❑ **Page Numbers** should be positioned "Bottom of page (Footer)" and Alignment "OUTSIDE." To begin page numbering you must first insert a SECTION BREAK on the last page prior to where you want page ONE to begin. In most cases page one is also the first page of Chapter One.

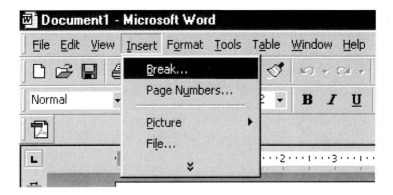

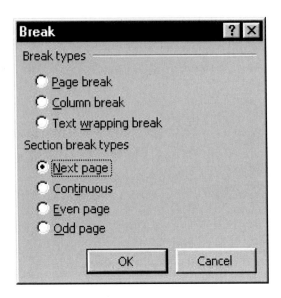

You want page ONE and all other ODD-NUMBERED pages to be right-hand pages, as in this book. Page ONE is always an ODD-NUMBERED and RIGHT-HAND page.

When working in *Microsoft Word*, this can be a bit confusing. A right-hand FACING page may appear on the left side of your screen when you are viewing the document at 75% or as TWO PAGES. This will become clearer if you put page numbers on the OUTSIDE. Page ONE will then have the page number on the right side of the page, making it a right-hand page. If page ONE is a left-hand page, simply insert a PAGE BREAK before the SECTION BREAK. Remember, you are creating a book, so think as though you had the book lying open in front of you on the table.

❑ **View Header and Footer.**

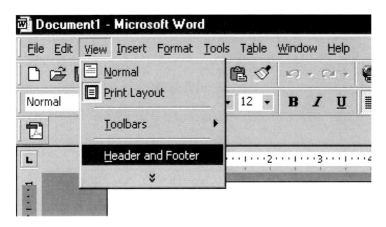

❑ **Then, Insert Page Numbers.**

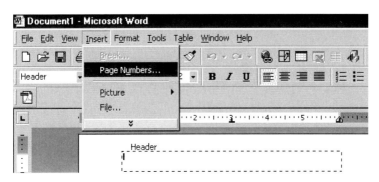

21

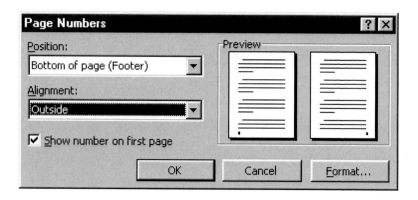

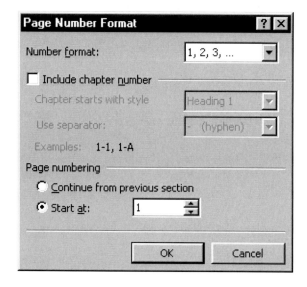

❑   **Chapter Titles and/or Sections** are in 12-point BOLD Font (Example: **Chapter 1**, etc.) and are CENTERED.

Each chapter should begin on its own RIGHT-HAND page. This often requires adding a blank page at the end of a chapter in order to make the next chapter begin on a RIGHT-HAND page. If you choose not to adhere to the right-hand Chapter starts, however, that is acceptable to us.

Once you put your book into the template, shown in Appendix A, this will all become clearer.

❑ **Table of Contents:** Please double-check the page numbers in your Table of Contents to ensure that they match the corresponding page numbers in the text. The Table of Contents should be a right-hand page also. If your Table of Contents extends past one page, have it start on a LEFT-HAND page so that when the book is open you can view the entire Table of Contents at once.

❑ **About the Author** should be the last page of text in your book.

❑ **Footnotes** may be a problem in some cases. If in doubt please use end notes.

❑ **Tables, Charts, and Images** may be inserted into your book. We highly recommend that you use the best quality images possible.

Images are less susceptible to conversion problems. So if at all possible scan them and save them as TIFF or JPEG images and then insert them into the document. Bookstand Publishing does not charge extra for images, tables, or charts. However, all internal art will be published as grayscale. This means that every photo, etc., will appear in shades of gray, not in full color. Consider this when you are placing photos in your book. See our full-color publishing packages for full-color-interior books.

❑ **Typos and Grammatical Mistakes:** As the author, you are responsible for fixing typographical and grammatical errors before your book is submitted. Errors fixed AFTER the proof file is submitted and the book is printed are subject to an editing fee.

❑ **Covers and Binding:** Our basic and most popular publishing service uses perfect binding. Perfect binding is commonly known as paperback or soft cover with a flat spine. The cover stock will be 80-lb. laminated cover stock, which allows for full-color printing of the highest quality. The cover graphics need to be provided by you. All paperback books are perfect-bound with a hot glue process. This creates a book comparable to the highest quality trade paperbacks found in any bookstore.

We also offer hardcover packages that use case binding. The result is a hardback book. Case binding is beautiful, with gold lettering on the spine and a full-color dusk jacket. It is a more intricate process than other types of binding. Our case-bound books can be produced in either blue or gray cloth.

❑ You can send your file to us in several ways:

    o Upload it through our website when you register. You will be given the option to upload your book immediately after choosing and paying for your book package.

    o E-mail it as an attachment if the file is not too large for your e-mail service provider.

    o FTP (File Transfer Protocol) directly to our server. This means you can "upload" the file somewhat like you move files on your home computer.

    o U.S. Mail. You can send us your file on a CD, thumb/flash drive, or secure digital media card via the U.S. Mail with prior approval from our staff. Using the Mail slows down the process considerably, however, as well as poses the risk of us receiving damaged disks, which would result in the entire submission process having to be repeated.

    ❑ Please contact us if you have questions.

ઠ **7** ભ

Distribution

Within 3 days of your final approval of your book, your self-published book will be available on your e-commerce page on www.bookstandpublishing.com.

Our regular book packages (all of them except the JumpStart Package) will have your book available through most major online bookstores within 4 to 5 weeks. These online bookstores include:

- Amazon.com US, UK, DE, JP
- BarnesandNoble.com
- Powells.com

Your book will also be available through Ingram and Baker and Taylor, the largest book wholesalers in the United States. In addition, your book will be registered with Bowkers Books In Print, which will enable your book to be special-ordered through most "brick-and-mortar" bookstores such as Borders and Barnes and Noble.

Self-Publishing Facts:

Author of a previous bestseller, *Permission Marketing*, Seth Godin turned down a generous offer from Simon & Schuster and self-published his book *Unleashing the Ideavirus*. First, though, he gave away the book on the Internet, including a tell-a-friend link. More than 200,000 people downloaded the book from his website alone; another 300,000 were exposed to his book from other websites. He then self-published it as a $40 hardcover. Within a week, he was #5 on the Amazon.com bestseller list. Twenty weeks after writing the book, he had exposed it to more than half a million people and had already begun making a profit on selling the printed book.

ᗏ 8 ᘓ

Promoting Your Book
What to Do <u>Before</u> Your Book is Published

If you are serious about marketing and promoting your self-published book, there are four questions you should ask yourself and answer <u>before</u> you submit your book for publication:

1. Who is my most probable customer for this book?
2. Why should my most probable customer want to buy my book?
3. What do I have to say to my most probable customer to make them want to buy my book?
4. How do I reach my most probable customer?

Answering these questions will help you think like a marketer and will lay the groundwork for implementing The 10 Step Marketing Plan, which follows in the next chapter. These questions should be answered before you publish your book because, as you will see, answering these questions can impact your book's title, description, and more. You don't want to decide, after your book has been published, that your book's title or description on the cover needs to be changed.

Let's examine each of these marketing questions.

1. Who is my most probable customer for this book?

You need to identify the most probable customer for your book. You need to do this so you can then target these people in your marketing and promotional efforts. While it may be tempting to believe that the whole world will want your book, from a marketing perspective you need to focus on the people who will most likely actually buy your book. You need to identify the demographics (that is, the objective facts) about your most probable customer. These demographics need to include at least some of the following information:

> Age
> Occupation
> Employment Status
> Income
> Location
> Gender
> Education
> Race/Ethnicity
> Marital Status
> Family Status
> Religion

Once you have this information, you are ready to answer the second marketing question:

2. Why should my most probable customer want to buy my book?

Now you want to get into the head of your most probable customer. What motivates them? When they buy your book, what are they expecting to get out of it? Are they seeking information? If so, what kind? Are they seeking excitement? If so, what kind of excitement? Are they seeking escape? How so? You are attempting here to understand the emotional psychology, or the psychographic profile, of your most probable reader.

Your answer to this question should be no more than one or two sentences long. Answering it will help you to answer the third question:

3. What do I have to say to my most probable customer to make them want to buy my book?

Your focus here is to determine what you need to say to your customer with:

> Your Title:
> Your Title needs to appeal to your most probable customer.

Your Book Description:
Your Book Description will, typically, go on the back of your book as well as appear on the websites of online retail stores across the country. It is this description that people will read first in deciding to buy your book. Thus, it needs to be complete and to appeal to your most probable customer.

Your Book Cover:
While we have always been taught that you shouldn't judge a book by its cover, the reality is that books are constantly being judged by their covers. As a result, you need to be sure that your cover strongly appeals to your most probable customer. Your book cover will be seen by anyone looking for your book, and so it needs to be compelling to your most probable customer.

Reviews:
It is great if you can get an advance review for your book before it is actually published. This review will be based upon your unpublished manuscript, and the review should be written by someone whom your probable customer looks up to. Once the book is published, of course, you should still seek reviews using the review copies of the book that come with your package; but advance reviews will be very helpful in marketing your book right out the gate.

4. How do I reach my most probable customer?

After you have identified a title that appeals to your most probable customer, produced a book description and book cover compelling to your most probable customer, and obtained any advance reviews, you need to make a list of how you can reach your most probable customer. That is, you need to make a list of the magazines they read, the websites they visit, and the stores they go to. The demographic profile you produced with Question 1 and the psychographic profile with Question 2 will help you answer this question.

Armed with the answers to these four marketing questions, you are ready to publish your book and begin implementing The 10 Step Marketing Plan. Before we turn to The 10 Step Marketing Plan, however, let's take a look at an example of applying these four marketing questions to a hypothetical book so you can better see how answering these questions could apply in your situation.

Example of Marketing Questions Applied:

Let's say you have written a book on White Water River Rafting. It is drawn from your 10 years of experiences as a white water river guide in the Pacific Northwest. It is a compilation of advanced techniques for running challenging rivers. It includes safety tips, information on reading rivers, and how to plan a river rafting trip in the Pacific Northwest.

Here is how you might answer the questions:

1. Who is my most probable customer for this book?

Profile:
Age 18 to 30 (White water rafting is predominantly a young person's sport)
Location: Washington State, Idaho, Montana, Oregon
Gender: Male (Rafting is predominantly a man's sport)
Marital Status: Single
Income: $35,000 +

2. Why should my most probable customer want to buy my book?

These young men are seeking thrills and adventure through white water rafting and are looking for ways to increase their thrills and adventure.

3. What do I have to say to my most probable customer to make them want to buy my book?

Title:
White Water! The Thrill and the Skill of Rafting the Greatest Rivers in the Pacific Northwest (I think this is a more appealing title to my most probable customer than just *White Water Rafting*)

Book Description:
An exciting and compelling white water rafting guide for anyone seeking the next level in their white water river adventures. Includes profiles of the best river challenges in the Pacific Northwest.

Book Cover:
Image of a rafter in dangerous white water rapids

Reviews:
Possible advance review from John Smith, current president of the Northwest Whitewater Association.

4. How do I reach my most probable customer?

Magazines;
> *Outdoor Life*
> *Adventure*

Websites:
> http://northwestwhitewater.org/
> www.whitewaterrafting.com
> www.raftingamerica.com/
> www.raftinfo.com/

Stores:
> My Guide Store
> Local REIs
> Sam's Rafting Store

Self-Publishing Facts:

Ken Blanchard and Spencer Johnson originally self-published *The One-Minute Manager* so they could sell the book for $15.00. All of the experts told them that they'd never sell such a short book for such a high price. In a three-month period of time, however, they sold more than 20,000 copies in the San Diego area alone — and then sold the reprint rights. More than 12 million copies have been sold since 1982, in more than 25 languages.

ஐ **9** ଔ

Promoting Your Book
The 10 Step Marketing Plan

Books do not sell themselves; they need to be promoted. The10 Step Marketing Plan gives you a good overview of what needs to be considered in promoting your book once it is published.

Upon the publication of your book, we will send you an updated copy of The 10 Step Marketing Plan, but we believe it best to share it with you now. This way, you can see what is involved and thereby better plan your promotional efforts up front.

Here are the Plan's 10 Steps:

1.   Always Be Selling

To sell books, you need to be always selling. Here is what you should do as soon as your book is published:

First, be sure to inform everyone you know that you have just published a book. Email them. Call them. Mention it in your Holiday cards. Place your book in a conspicuous location on your desk at work. You get the idea.

Second, create positive excitement by giving away some books to your friends and colleagues in exchange for their giving you positive reviews that you can use in your marketing efforts. You can also ask them to post positive reviews on Amazon.com and, if they have a blog, you can ask them to blog about your book.

Third, you may want to consider creating Bookmarks and Business Cards that feature your book's cover and provide your web page or Bookstand Publishing e-commerce page address, so you can create interest and conveniently let people know where to go to buy your book. You can also create a Postcard that you can send to your contacts and use in your marketing efforts. You may purchase these items at www.colorpostcards.com or you can purchase them through Bookstand Publishing at www.bookstandpublishing.com/marketing_services.php

Finally, you should create an effective sell sheet. You might consider preparing and distributing your sell sheet to book buyers and wholesalers. Comparable in purpose to a press release, a sell sheet is a one-page written flyer-type piece that includes pertinent information about your book, along with a thumbnail photo of your book in the top left corner. The photo serves to put the image of your book's cover in the hands, and minds, of buyers as well as consumers.

In your sell sheet, include a synopsis; an author's bio; basic facts about the book, such as its ISBN, price, number of pages, dimensions, and formats available; reviews or quotes from readers or reviewers; and important marketing information.

The sell sheet may either be inserted in a media kit or distributed independently as a complement to a press release.

Bookstand Publishing can help you develop your sell sheet. Just go to www.bookstandpublishing.com/marketing_services.php

2.   Get Reviews

Reviews sell books. The better the reviews, the more books you sell. The more reviews, the more books you sell.

Here is what you need to do:

First, once your book is live on Amazon.com, have your friends and associates post at least three positive reviews about your book. Three or more reviews will provide a good picture of your book, and will allow customers to determine if yours is a book they want.

Second, send copies of your book to the organizations below. Most of them will review your book for FREE. Some of them are "fee for review" organizations, which means they will charge you a fee to do a book review. The reviews are posted on their web sites and on Amazon.com, and you can use them in your promotional materials:

- www.bookreview.com: They will want one copy of your book. If you want to expedite the review, you may want to consider their Express Review Service for a fee.
- www.midwestbookreview.com: They will want two copies of your book as well as a cover letter and a press release.
- www.lightwordreviews.com/submit-work.html: They review only non-fiction books and will require one copy of your book. www.oncewritten.com/About/GettingYourBookReviewed.php: Free online recommendations.
- www.forewordmagazine.com/clarion/: This is a review for fee service.
- www.kirkusdiscoveries.com/kirkusreviews/discoveries/index.jsp: This is another review for fee service.

Third, send review copies of your book, together with a cover letter that includes your contact information and your personal Bookstand Publishing order webpage address, to "high value" media prospects. We recommend that you send review copies with a cover letter to the following:

- Local newspapers (local small town newspapers work best since you are now a local author).
- Specialized magazines your target audience reads. You may want to consult *Writers Market* or www.writersmarket.com for a list and description of all the specialized magazines that may be of interest to your target market.
- Specialized website your target market reads.
- Local libraries.
- Appropriate universities and colleges if your book has the potential to become required reading for a given topic or subject in a course or courses.

After this, you may want to consider distributing an electronic press release. Here are some companies that can help you perform a "Press Release blast":

- www.PRweb.com

- Bookstand Publishing. We can both prepare and distribute a press release for you. Just go to www.bookstandpublishing.com/marketting_services.php and click on Press Release Preparation. We can also distribute your press release electronically with two different programs.

One additional service you may want to consider is www.prleads.com. For a fee of $99 a month they can put you in touch with reporters who are looking for stories and quotes from experts like you. You have to be an expert in your field, however, and they have to accept you as a client.

3. Your Website

You already have a Bookstand Publishing e-commerce web page; and this might be the only web page you wish to have. If so, all of your online promotion should direct potential customers to your Bookstand Publishing e-commerce web page.

However, if you already have a website of your own, then you should add a place on your site in which to promote your book, and add a "Buy Now" button that links to your personal e-commerce web page URL on Bookstand Publishing's website so you do not have to go to the expense of setting up your own e-commerce website. In this case, your existing website should become the web address you promote.

If you don't have a website, you may want to consider developing a small website exclusively to promote your book. This can be done quite inexpensively; and, by adding a "Buy Now" button linking to your personal URL on Bookstand Publishing, you will not have to incur the expense of setting up your own e-commerce website. If you do set up your new website, you should use its address as the web address you promote. The advantages of having your own website to promote your book include:

- An easy to remember unique domain name (e.g., www.mygreatbook.com).
- A stronger professional image.

- Additional pages that the search engines can pick up to better lead people to your book.
- A lot more space to talk about your book, and related topics.
- Through Google Analytics (www.google.com/analytics) or other tracking services, you can track where your traffic is coming from and modify your marketing efforts accordingly.

A simple website can be created quite inexpensively. Here are some options to consider:

- www.Web.com: Their do-it-yourself website builder is only $11.95 a month and includes a domain name.
- www.AmericanAuthor.com: Provides a very nice professional website for authors for a $399 set up fee and $29.95 a month.
- www.WebHostingForAuthors.com: For $4.99 a month you can have a five-page website that can be built from one of their pre-built templates. Just go to this site and click on the Website Tonight service. WebHostingForAuthors.com is owned by Bookstand Publishing.

4.   On-line Promotion

Most books today are sold on the web and not through "brick and mortar" bookstores. You thus need to generate awareness of your book on the web and drive traffic to your e-commerce page or website as well as other online channels such as Amazon.com and BarnesandNoble.com.

Here are some inexpensive (mostly free) ways you can drive traffic on the web towards your book:

"Listmania":

Post a Listmania on Amazon.com. Your Listmania should be a list of similar books to yours and include your book. For example, if you wrote a book on white water rafting, you should create a Listmania of your favorite white water rafting books, being sure to include your new book on the list. This will allow customers who are already reading the other white water rafting books to become aware of your book. You can add a Listmania here:
www.amazon.com/gp/richpub/listmania/createpipelin

"Find Similar Books":

You may want to consider writing reviews for other books similar to yours on Amazon.com, and referencing your book in your review. You can do the equivalent on other online stores and sites. For example, if you wrote a book on white water rafting you might write a review and add, "I really liked this book on white water rafting. It is my favorite along with my book, [*TITLE OF YOUR BOOK*], and I think both are essential reading for the white water rafter." The key here is to create awareness of your book among the people who will be the most interested in it. This is easy to do on Amazon.com and BarnesandNoble.com.

Create a Blog:

A well done blog can drive a lot of traffic to your e-commerce page or web page. A blog is where you can post your thoughts, excerpts from your book, and your experiences for others to read. You will, of course, want to include a link to you webpage on your blog. You can set up your blog for free or for a small cost. You will need to spend some time regularly adding new material, however, as that is what drives traffic. Here are some sites that can help you set up your blog:

- www.blogger.com: Sets up a blog for free.
- www.wordpress.com: Sets up a blog for free.
- www.WebHostingForAuthors.com: The Quick Blogcast service offered by Bookstand Publishing's sister company, WebHostingForAuthors.com, begins at only $4.99 a month. This site has many handy tools to help you set up a blog.

Email:

E-newsletters and professional advertising done via email can drive traffic to your webpage. Here are some sites that can help you in setting up and sending your emails:

- www.ConstantContact.com: This site includes some good suggestions on how to build your email lists.
- www.Icontact.com.
- www.resultsmail.com.
- www.WebHostingForAuthors.com: The Express Email Marketing service offered by Bookstand Publishing's sister company begins at only $7.99 a month.

Also: Always reference your book in your email signatures.

Social Networking:

Social networking drives traffic. The best social networks are the ones your target market uses. Some FREE social networking sites you might consider:
- www.goodreads.com: Site for book lovers.
- www.bookcrossing.com.
- www.shelfari.com: You can show off your books here too.
- www.librarything.com.
- www.authorsden.com: A free online community of authors and readers.
- www.selfpublishersplace.com/.
- www.authorsonthenet.com/: An online blog for authors.
- www.facebook.com: One of the most popular social networking sites. Many businesses and authors use this site to promote their books .

Cross Linking:

You should seek out web sites that your target market visits and suggest that the site offer a link to your site in exchange for you linking to them. Do a Google search for your book topic and see what new sites you find that your target market might be visiting. Some of these sites may be good choices for advertising if such is in your budget.

YouTube:

If you have a video that promotes your book or yourself, post it on YouTube at www.youtube.com to help draw traffic to your web page.

<u>Search Engine Advertising</u>:

You can set up a Google Ad Words account (http://adwords.google.com) based on key words to drive traffic to your site. You can set this up such that you can be sure you don't exceed your budget. For example, if your budget is $25 a month, you can set it up so that once your budget has been reached you aren't charged anything more for the month. Google Analytics (www.google.com/analytics) is FREE and allows you to track the results of your campaign.

Yahoo! and other search engines offer similar Ad Word programs that you may also want to consider.

5. Book Signings

Request local bookstores to allow you to hold a book signing in their stores. Once your book signing is scheduled, place a "Local Author Book Signing" ad in your local papers to advertise the event. Also, be sure to ask what advertising the bookstore will do for you. At the signing, you sign each book, and the bookstore can sell it and take a royalty. Plan ahead so that you have enough books on hand. Keep track of how many books you sign, and at the end of the signing do the accounting with the bookstore.

Bookstore chains like Borders and Barnes and Noble will typically insist on ordering your book through Ingram or Baker & Taylor, but independent bookstores may work with you directly from your own inventory of books. Typically, bookstores are looking for a 35% to 55% cut of book signing sales. Generally, independent bookstores are easier to work with in setting up a book signing than the chain stores; and, unlike the chains, are usually eager to have you set up a book signing.

Request your local libraries to host book signings. Here, you will need to bring your own copies of your book and sell them on a cash basis.

You might also consider hosting a book signing at your place of business.

6. Special Events

Topic-Related Events:

If your book covers a niche subject, such as "White Water Rafting for Seniors," then look for events involving that subject, such as white water rafting tours for seniors. In this example, you should market your book to white water rafting companies nationwide; request white water rafting stores to carry your book; request white water rafting supply catalogs to offer your book; seek out white water rafting websites that would link to your book for purchase; attend white water rafting conventions, and have a booth as a vendor to sell your book; contact the white water rafting associations, purchase their mailing lists, and send postcards about your book to their members; and ask the white water rafting organizations to offer your book as a bonus for membership in their organizations (this could generate large orders from these organizations).

In short, look for areas that have synergy with your book and market to them. Sometimes they will want consignment and other times they may place a large order of 500 or more books to distribute.

Annual Book Fairs:

Most large metropolitan areas have annual book fairs, and these are usually great places for local authors to promote their books.

7. Speaking Engagements

If you are an expert in a specific field, and your book ties in with your expertise, and you are currently giving public talks, you should definitely sell your book at your speaking engagements. For example, if you are selling a book on white water rafting, and you regularly speak on the topic of white water rafting, you should begin selling your books wherever you speak. Nothing sells books better than a talk followed by an opportunity to buy the speaker's books.

If you aren't already giving public talks related to your area of expertise/book topic, you should consider doing so to promote your book. You may want to consider offering to speak to relevant associations, clubs, church groups, political organizations, etc., for free and make your book available for purchase in the latter portion of the event. Your book sales could pay for your time spent speaking.

8. Business Tie-ins

If you have an existing business and your book ties in with your business, you should sell your book through your business. There are several ways to do this:

Require your clients to purchase your book as a part of the service you offer. For example, if you offer instructional classes on white water river rafting, you could require you students to purchase your book on white water rafting, or you could raise the price of your classes a bit and include your book for "free."

You could also take a different approach and offer your book to potential clients as a lead in to a bigger sale. For example, you might offer your book to customers who are considering taking your white water rafting classes with the view that they will read the book and then be more likely to pay the tuition for your classes. You won't make money on book sales if you give away your books, of course, but if doing so increases your sales conversions to your main business, then a book giveaway can still be a money maker for you.

If you own a store, you can offer your book at the point of purchase. For example, if you own a sporting goods store, you could offer your white water rafting book at the point of purchase (i.e., in front of the Cash Register).

As another example, if you offer counseling sessions, and your book is relevant to that field, put your book on a bookstand with pricing and ordering information so that all of your counseling clients see it.

You may also want to hold a book signing at your place of business. The fact is that your existing clients are the best prospects to purchase your book.

9. Sell to Local Bookstores, Gift Shops, and Other Local Vendors

You should try selling wholesale copies of your book directly to local vendors. Go to local bookstores and see if they will carry your book. Be aware, however, that it is tough to sell to chain bookstores like Borders and Barnes and Noble because they often don't want to deal with unknown authors. Moreover, they will demand a 35% to 55% cut of your book's retail price for each copy sold, and they will only purchase your book through Ingram or Baker & Taylor. Independent, locally owned bookstores are much easier to deal with, and may purchase books directly from your inventory of books. This means more profits for you. Typically, chain bookstores are looking for a 35% to 55% cut of the sale, and they will only take your book on consignment (i.e., they will return any unsold books to you). Museums and gift shops at historical points of interest also work well if your book is about a specific location or individual of local or relevant interest. These organizations will typically only sell your book on consignment.

As we mentioned under the Special Events section (#6 above), selling your books at topic-related events and local book fairs affords excellent opportunities to promote and sell your book.

You can purchase your book wholesale through the Bookstand Publishing wholesale order system. Each order must be for a quantity of 25 or more copies. Go to www.BookstandPublishing.com, log in to your Author Login, and go to the wholesale tab. Wholesale author orders are typically 50% or more below the retail price.

10. Advertising

If you can afford it, you may want to consider advertising for your book. Generally we recommend that you try advertising in the following order to keep your budget under control:

1. Online advertising
   - Google Ad Words.
   - Banner advertising on a niche site related to your book topic.
   - Email advertising on a niche site related e-zine.

2. Specialized print publications that reach your specific target market.

   If per our example above you are selling a white water rafting book, you will do better placing an ad in a white water rafting magazine than in the *New York Times* (you will save a lot of money too). Don't buy a big ad initially; instead, start by buying a small ad. If it works, then buy the big ad. Advertising in print publications can be very expensive, so be prudent in how you spend and budget your money.

   You may want to consult *Writers Market* or www.writersmarket.com to obtain a list and descriptions of all of the specialized publications that might be of interest to your target market.

3. Book Trade Catalogs

   Book wholesalers such as Ingram and Baker & Taylor will sell advertising space in their trade catalogs, which are distributed to bookstores and distributors. They have many catalog categories ranging from general trade catalogs to specialty catalogs. Be careful, though, as this advertising can be expensive. Bookstand Publishing will need to assist you with this type of advertising, as Ingram and Baker & Taylor will require that you go through your publisher. Let us know if this avenue of advertising interests you, and we will obtain pricing for you. However, be prepared to spend a minimum of $1,000 for this type of advertising.

Always remember to budget your advertising, and pull any advertising that doesn't work immediately. Also, don't sign any long-term contracts until you know that a particular form or avenue of advertising is working for you.

ℬ **10** ℭ

Promoting Your Book
What Do I Do with 48 Books?

Most of our paperback packages include 48 copies of your book. These copies are provided so that you can effectively promote and market your book.

Here is a sample outline of how you can use your 48 books to promote your book following the guidelines in the 10 Step Marketing Plan:

1. Copies for family and friends (be sure you get at least some of these people to agree to post favorable reviews on Amazon.com and elsewhere in exchange for the free book): 15 copies

2. Copies to send for reviews:
www.bookreview.com	1 copy
www.midwestbookreview.com	2 copies
www.lightwordreviews.com	1 copy
www.oncewritten.com	1 copy
Local newspapers, with press release	2 copies
Targeted magazines, with press release	3 copies
Target web sites, with press release	3 copies
Total Review:	13 copies

3. Copies for distribution at local bookstores, or gift shops (on a consignment basis): 5 copies

4. Copies for sales at book signings at local bookstores or speaking engagements 15 copies

Total 48 copies

Self-Publishing Facts:

Amanda Brown used First Books to self-publish her first novel *Legally Blonde* as a print-on-demand book. Her self-published book was made into a movie starring Reese Witherspoon. A year and a half after the movie was made, Plume published her book, with an additional chapter on what's next for Elle Woods. Plume will also publish the sequel, *Red, White & Blonde*. In the meantime, Dutton will be publishing a hardcover of another novel, *Family Trust*, which has already been optioned for a movie by Hillary Swank and Chad Lowe.

❧ **11** ☙

Questions to Ask Yourself
Before You Choose a Publisher

1. How long has the company been providing publishing services?

Bookstand Publishing has been helping authors publish their books in trade paperback and Adobe Acrobat eBook formats since 1996. Bookstand Publishing has numerous titles in its catalog. Today, in addition to trade paperback printed books, you can have your book printed in blue or gray cloth case-bound hardcover format with a full-color dust jacket.

2. Can my printed book be less than 108 pages long?

If you have a shorter book, Bookstand Publishing can publish it. In fact, we can publish a trade paperback with as few as 15 pages, and a hardcover with as few as 50.

3. What if I'm not a computer expert?

We understand that not all authors are computer experts, so we make the process of preparing your book easier for you. We provide all of the step-by-step instructions for creating your book on our web site. Furthermore, we include this information in the book you're reading now, *The Self-Publishing Checklist*.

Every setup/production fee includes professional layout services. We can also take a printed book and have it made into an electronic file. There is an additional fee for this service.

4. How can I obtain a customized, unique finished book?

Bookstand Publishing believes that each author's work is unique and original, and that it should be treated as such during the production process. When you publish with Bookstand Publishing, your manuscript is given to a page design professional who will give your book that finished quality you expect.

This personalized attention carries through to the custom cover design for your book. Each Bookstand Publishing book cover is custom-designed by a professional artist. If you choose instead to go with one of our existing template covers, your book's data (title, your name, etc.) will be added to it.

5. How can I get a fair percentage of all book sales?

Bookstand Publishing offers one of the highest royalty rates in the industry. We pay 30% of the retail price when a customer purchases your book directly from our web site, www.bookstandpublishing.com. This is a full 10% to 20% higher than many other print-on-demand publishers pay. For books sold via bookstores and not through our web site, Bookstand Publishing pays 15%. For books sold through our Alibris channels, we pay 10% of the retail price. On eBook sales, we pay you from 30% to 50% of the retail price, depending upon the sales channel.

It is important to note that many print-on-demand publishers pay a percentage based upon the wholesale price of the book. In contrast, Bookstand Publishing pays all royalties based upon the **retail** price of the book.

6. What rights must I give up in order to publish my book via print-on-demand?

With Bookstand Publishing, you retain **all rights**. Whether you publish your book in print or eBook form, you retain all rights. Our agreement is also non-exclusive. This means you can take your title to other distributors, bookstores, and publishers. Your book is **yours**; **you own it**. We are simply offering you a service to help you succeed at *making a living selling your writing.*

7. Is the publishing contract I am asked to sign fair and complete?

Bookstand Publishing prides itself on presenting a comprehensive, complete, and easy-to-understand publishing agreement to our authors, with no fine print.

We clearly define the following:

- You retain all rights to your work.
- The time frame of the publishing agreement.
- The percentage of the retail price paid to you from any resulting sales.
- When earnings from sales of your book are paid to you .
- The exact production specifications of your finished book.

All of Bookstand Publishing's contract details are clearly presented on our web site.

Before you sign any publishing agreement with any publisher, be sure that all of the details are clear to you.

Self-Publishing Facts:

Judith Appelbaum originally self-published *How to Get Happily Published*, then sold the rights to Harper Collins. The book has now been through many editions and has sold more than 500,000 copies.

❧ **12** ☙

Common Questions about Bookstand Publishing's Print-on-Demand Services

1. Are you a vanity publisher?

No. We are not the publisher, you are. Bookstand Publishing will provide you with the tools necessary for you to publish and sell your work. Think of it this way: We provide you with the VEHICLE; you have to DRIVE the sales to the web page that we set up for you. We are book printers, e-commerce providers, and eBook experts. We help you succeed.

2. Can I print a book in a language other than English?

Not a problem. Simply make sure your book is delivered to Bookstand Publishing in print-ready Adobe Acrobat format. We have published titles in Taiwanese, Spanish, Russian, German, and Italian, in addition to English.

3. What can Bookstand Publishing do for me?

When you register as an author with Bookstand Publishing, you become part of our family. At Bookstand Publishing, we have established a goal: To give every author the best possible chance at success. We will thus make every effort to help you become successful.

We set up a home page for you and your book. On your home page you will find that we list your e-mail address. With your e-mail address posted, other interested parties and other publishers can contact you directly. We will never stand in the way of your success. In contrast, look at our competition: Some print-on-demand publishers seem to make direct contact with authors impossible.

We offer you a very attractive **wholesale price** on your books. Our prices are very competitive, and we only require that you purchase a minimum of 25 copies of your book in order to receive the maximum discount. Our price schedule can be found on our website at www.bookstandpublishing.com.

As sales are made, you are e-mailed a copy of each sales order, showing the customer and the book title so that, over time, you can develop a marketing plan based upon past purchasers. You are also assigned an online account that you can access to see your on-going sales. You will be paid each month for those sales credited to the previous month.

4. What won't Bookstand Publishing do for me?

We do not act as your agent or public relations firm. We are a fulfillment company that will give you the tools necessary for you to promote and sell your book. The more effort you put into selling your book, the more rewards you will see. Printing one copy of your book and placing it in your local library will not by itself give you satisfactory returns (although doing so is a good marketing idea).

The old saying, "A book stops selling when the author does," is true. You are a self-published author. As such, your book's success or failure is entirely in your hands. However, Bookstand Publishing can help you considerably in making your book a success.

5. What about the eBook Price?

If your book is an eBook, we highly recommend that you price your book so it is competitive. In order to be competitive in eBook form, your book must sell for less than $10.00 in most cases, unless your book contains highly technical and valuable information. The most widely accepted price for an eBook today is $9.95. We will recommend a price range, but the final decision as to your book's price is yours.

If you choose a given price but wish to change it in the future, contact support@bookstandpublishing.com and we will do so at no charge.

6. What format can I submit my book in?

You can send us work in *Microsoft Word* files with an extension of ".doc" (".docx" in *Word 2007*), or in Adobe PDF. For *Works 4.0*, *WordPerfect*, or other word processing application formats, please contact us prior to registration. We can handle most conversions, but some costs may apply.

If you are using an Apple Macintosh (Mac) computer, contact the nearest Kinko's copy center. For less than $10.00, Kinko's will convert your Mac file to a PDF file for us. Please note that your MAC file must be formatted to our specifications BEFORE you have it converted to a PDF file. Please contact us for more details.

PDF files should be "Press Optimized" and all fonts embedded.

We have a free *Word* template in various trim sizes that you can use. The 5.25-inch x 8.25-inch template is available at:
http://www.bookstandpublishing.com/free/POD_template.doc

7. Can you help me format my manuscript for publishing?

As indicated in Question #6, we have a free *Word* template in various trim sizes that you can use. The 5.25-inch x 8.25-inch template is available at:
http://www.bookstandpublishing.com/free/POD_template.doc

8. What about pictures?

We encourage photos or drawings as long as they are part of the document. Black-and-white images are fine at any location in the book. If you want to insert limited **color** images in your book, they will print in grayscale unless you purchase a full-color package where every page can have color.

You must be aware of a graphics term called "RESOLUTION" when dealing with images. The resolution of an image is measured in DOTS PER INCH, abbreviated as dpi. A print-quality image must be 300 dpi or higher. As an example, the images located in the Checklist portion of this book are only 72 dpi. Images taken from the Web are also 72 dpi in most cases. When scanning images, you must set the scanner resolution option for 300 dpi minimum. Although screenshots reproduce nicely, detailed photos need to be 300 dpi or else they will appear quite fuzzy.

As the dpi increases, however, so does the file size. So don't be surprised if you scan an image at 300 dpi and the file size jumps by 20 megabytes. File size is not an issue until you want to move the file from your computer to another. You must have the ability to BURN a CD, a memory card, a jump drive, or a thumb drive. If you do not have that capability, you will be confronted with having your wonderful piece of work stuck on your computer, with no way to move it.

Please note: Picture size and number of pictures will affect the "download ability" of your book when it is in eBook form. If your primary goal is to sell printed books and not eBooks, though, then this issue should not concern you.

9. What categories of books may I submit to Bookstand Publishing?

We will accept all works that are in good taste. We will not accept pornography. We will not accept any books that promote hate, or the overthrowing of any government.

10. Can I submit my book to others also?

Yes. When you submit your work to Bookstand Publishing, we have a non-exclusive license. This means you can submit your work to print publishers, to our competitors, and even to movie companies, if you wish. Remember: Your book is yours, and we are here as a resource to help you, not to hinder you.

11. Should I copyright my work?

Your manuscript has a form of copyright protection from the moment that you create it. To provide an official record, it is advisable to submit your manuscript to the United States Copyright office. Remember, you receive 48 copies of your book, and only two are needed for the copyright process.

See www.loc.gov/copyright for a more detailed explanation. Or contact http://www.clickandcopyright.com/

12. What is an ISBN?

The International Standard Book Number (**ISBN**) is a 10-digit number that uniquely identifies books and book-like products published internationally.

The purpose of the ISBN is to establish and identify one title or edition of a title from one specific publisher and is unique to that edition, allowing for more efficient marketing of products by booksellers, libraries, universities, wholesalers, and distributors. For more information and application go to:
www.isbn.org/standards/home/isbn/us/application.html

13. Do I need an ISBN?

Yes. We include one on each **printed title** at no additional cost to the author.

If you have this number already, please advise us. You can include it on the book and in the web page we create for you. We also supply an EAN bar code, with the price embedded, for the cover art.

14. How long does the process take to get my book into print?

Once you have given your final approval of the formatted PDF file we create for you, you will see the printed proof of your book in less than 10 days.

Experience tells us that it takes about two weeks to format, convert, edit, and print the proof. We urge you to have two friends review your book BEFORE it is ready to print. You don't want to prematurely approve your book for print, only to have an error jump out later once the book is already printed.

If you have an urgent need to have your book available and online by a specific date or time, please let us know and we will do everything we possibly can to accommodate you. Basically, our publishing process can take as little as five weeks from the submission of your book to the arrival of your 48 copies.

15. What if I want to update my book later?

We offer a file replacement service for both the book block and the cover art. For more information, please contact:
authorservices@bookstandpublishing.com

16. What if I don't have my manuscript on disk?

We have the ability to accurately scan hardcopy manuscripts and existing books. However, keep in mind that if you have a bound book, it will have to be taken apart to go through the scanning process. The book will thus be destroyed in the process, although the pages themselves will remain intact.

We suggest you consider using your local high school or college for the typing or scanning of your manuscript. Many educational institutions would love the opportunity for their students to obtain some real-world experience. You may even be able to have a journalism class edit your work. Often, these services are free. Check into this win-win situation to getting your book ready to publish.

17. What about the cover?

You can choose to create your own cover or have someone do it for you. The guidelines below will provide you with the necessary cover specifications.

Bookstand Publishing also offers an assortment of Theme, Basic and Deluxe Cover art designs that come FREE with your Publishing Package. Photos can be added to any of these designs for an additional fee. To preview the designs, visit:
www.bookstandpublishing.com/content/cover_art

Finally, Bookstand Publishing can design a custom cover for you to your exact specifications. Our current rate for a custom cover is $299.

All cover images must be TIFF or JPEG files in CMYK scheme and 300-dpi **minimum**. The greater the dpi, the greater the resolution and the better the cover will look.

Covers must be 0.250 inches larger than the finished size of the book. Thus, a 5.25-inch x 8.25-inch sized book requires cover art to be 5.5 inches x 8.5 inches. You should submit one file with all covers included. For example, the TIFF file must contain the Front, the Back, and the Spine, including the bleed.

To determine the "Spine Thickness" for a paperback book, take half the page count to determine the number of sheets of paper and multiply that by 0.0046" and add .010". For example, a 150-page book contains 75 sheets of paper. Thus, 75 x 0.0046" + .010" = 0.355", so the spine thickness is 0.355 inch.

Make sure that you and/or your graphic artist understand the specifications BEFORE you create your cover.

Below are a few samples of our available template cover art.

Sample Deluxe Cover Templates

Sample Basic Cover Templates
(These templates can be customized by adding a photo
or changing the background color)

Each cover design will include a standard ISBN bar code on the back cover, along with the category classification, a summary, and, if space permits, the author's biography.

The cover samples above are only a few of the templates offered by Bookstand Publishing. You can view all of the examples in color, and in larger size, at:
www.bookstandpublishing.com/content/cover_art

❧ **13** ☙

How Do I Sign Up?

Go to www.bookstandpublishing.com/content/publishing

This explains in more detail the process and provides a list of the services that we provide at Bookstand Publishing.

When you are ready to proceed to become a writer with a published book, go to www.bookstandpublishing.com/author_sign_up.

You may also email your manuscript to andy@bookstandpublishing.com with your name and phone number. One of our staff members will review your manuscript, and give you a call and register you over the phone.

You may also call us at 866-793-9365 and we can discuss your publishing project.

Self-Publishing Facts:

Roger Price and Leonard Stern self-published an entire series of *Mad Libs* books that have sold almost 150 million copies and helped establish their publishing company, Price Stern Sloan (which they later sold to Penguin Putnam).

∾ **14** ☙

Self-Publishing Hall of Fame

If you are thinking about self-publishing your book, you're in good company. Check out this list of great writers who also self-published their books. This is but a very small list, as thousands of famous writers have self-published.

- Edgar Rice Burroughs
- Zane Grey
- Rudyard Kipling
- DH Lawrence
- Gertrude Stein
- Virginia Woolf

Mark Twain paid for the publication of *The Adventures of Huckleberry Finn* when he became tired of the foolishness of his previous publishers. He then invested the money earned from the sale of that book to help develop one of the first working typewriters.

Joe "Mr. Fire!" Vitale (http://www.mrfire.com/) has done it all. After having several books published by mainstream publishers, he became fed up with their poor marketing efforts, and self-published his succeeding books. *Turbocharge Your Writing* went through 13 editions and sold 25,000 copies. *The Seven Lost Secrets of Success* went through nine editions. One company so loved it that they purchased 19,500 copies of the book. And *Spiritual Marketing* is his #1 best-selling book on Amazon.com. That book sold 5,000 copies in one day, earned Joe a feature story in *The New York Times*, led to several publishers wanting to buy the book, led to foreign publishers wanting to translate it, and became the first print-on-demand book in history to become a #1 bestseller.

Russian count and novelist Leo Tolstoy paid 4,500 rubles for the first printing of his major novel, *War and Peace*, which is considered one of the greatest novels in world literature. His other major novel was *Anna Karenina*.

American poet and short story writer Edgar Allen Poe, author of the poem *The Raven* and short stories such as *The Tell-Tale Heart* and *The Fall of the House of Usher,* self-published some of his writings.

Business consultant Tom Peters self-published *In Search of Excellence* and sold more than 25,000 copies directly to consumers in the first year. He then sold the rights to Warner, whose edition has gone on to sell more than 10 million copies.

Robert Kiyosaki sold more than a million copies of his self-published *Rich Dad, Poor Dad* in less than three years. He went on to add several more major bestsellers in the series.

Irish author James Joyce, author of *Ulysses*, *Finnegans Wake*, and many other novels, paid for the printing of *Ulysses* in 1922 with the help of some of his friends. (This is called patronage publishing.)

French novelist Alexandre Dumas, author of such swashbuckling romances as *The Three Musketeers* and *The Count of Monte Cristo*, self-published some of his first books.

In 1951, Howard Fast couldn't find a publisher for his novel *Spartacus* because he was a member of the Communist Party and was therefore blacklisted at that time. As a result, he published the book himself. It became a bestseller and went on to be made into an incredible movie. In 1956, Fast broke with the Communist Party after revelations of Stalin-era atrocities came to light.

John Kremer, author and publisher of *1001 Ways to Market Your Books*, and developer of this chapter's Self-Publishing Hall of Fame, has helped thousands of authors and publishers to get their books on or near the bestseller lists. Indirectly, at the very least, he has inspired the sales of more than a billion books.

In 1939, Louis L'Amour privately published his first book, a collection of poems known as *Smoke from This Altar*. Years later the collection was republished by Bantam, and has gone on to sell more than 100,000 copies. More than 10 years after his poetry book was published, his first novel was published. His 100 westerns have sold more than 200 million copies worldwide, and 45 of his novels and short stories have been made into movies.

Brenda Ponichtera has done a wonderful job of promoting her *Quick & Healthy Cookbooks*, which have sold more than half a million copies.

British poet Alexander Pope, author of the satirical mock-epic poems *The Rape of the Lock* and *The Dunciad*, paid for the publication of his first book.

After publisher Frederick Warne rejected *The Tale of Peter Rabbit* because of the costs of printing the illustrations, Beatrix Potter self-published a limited edition of 250 copies in 1901. When Warne saw the finished book, he immediately recognized the book's commercial possibilities and brought out a commercial edition with color illustrations in 1902. To date the book has sold more than 40 million copies and been translated into 35 languages.

Melvin Powers, publisher of Wilshire Books, has self-published a number of his own titles on mail order marketing, self-publishing, and success. In addition, he has sold millions of copies of other authors' titles that his company publishes.

Dan Poynter self-published his classic *Self-Publishing Manual* in 1979 and has gone on to sell more than 130,000 copies over 16 editions. He calls it "the book that launched a thousand books."

Roger Price and Leonard Stern self-published an entire series of *Mad Libs* books that have sold almost 150 million copies and helped establish their publishing company, Price Stern Sloan (which they later sold to Penguin Putnam).

French author Marcel Proust paid to publish the first 1,500 pages of *Remembrance of Things Past*, his seven-part novel published between 1913 and 1927. His work is considered one of the greatest works of modern literature.

Irma Rombauer used $3,000 from her husband's estate to self-publish *The Joy of Cooking* in 1931. Since then, this cookbook has sold millions of copies. Today, more than 75 years later, it still sells more than 100,000 copies per year. In November 1997, Scribners published a completely revised fifth edition, the first new edition in 20 years. By early December 1997, the book had already made the bestseller lists with more than 750,000 copies in print.

Irish-born British playwright and author George Bernard Shaw started out as a jobbing printer who self-published some of his own work. He went on to write many famous plays, including *Pygmalion* and *Saint Joan*. In addition, he founded the Fabian Society and won the 1925 Nobel Prize for Literature.

John Muir founded the company that bears his name in order to self-publish his multi-million-copy bestseller, *How to Keep Your Volkswagen Alive*. The book still sells thousands of copies each year.

Victoria Christopher Murray, author of the novel *Temptation*, made the jump from self-publishing to being published by a major publisher.

Bill Myers self-published many videos, as well as several books and a newsletter on how to make and sell videos. He later sold the rights to many of these products, retired to New Zealand, and then returned to the United States to self-publish and market a line of software designed to make it easier to sell videos and other products via the Internet.

T.S. Eliot, author of *The Love Song of J. Alfred Prufrock* and *The Waste Land*, paid for the publication of his first book.

Cindy Cashman, with her then-partner Alan Garner, self-published *Everything Men Know About Women* (using the pseudonym of Dr. Alan Francis), and sold more than half a million copies of the blank book before selling rights to Andrews McMeel. The book has now sold more than a million copies. Many copies of the book were sold through Spencer's gift stores and women's clothing stores.

Scott Adams, creator of the *Dilbert* comic strip and book series, self-published an original eBook, *God's Debris*, early in 2001 as a way of testing the market for a new book. As a result, he was able to get an "unusually good deal" from his regular publisher, Andrews McMeel, when he sold them the book rights.

Judith Appelbaum originally self-published *How to Get Happily Published*, then sold the rights to Harper Collins. The book has now been through many editions and has sold more than 500,000 copies.

John Bartlett financed and published the first three editions of *Bartlett's Familiar Quotations*, the best-selling quotations book on the market.

L. Frank Baum self-published some of the books in the *Wizard of Oz* series.

Amanda Brown used First Books to self-publish her first novel, *Legally Blonde*, as a print-on-demand book. Her self-published book was made into a movie starring Reese Witherspoon. A year and a half after the movie was made, Plume published her book with an additional chapter on what's next for Elle Woods. Plume will also publish the sequel, *Red, White & Blonde*. In the meantime, Dutton will be publishing a hardcover edition of another of Brown's novels, *Family Trust*, which has already been optioned for a movie by Hillary Swank and Chad Lowe.

H. Jackson Brown originally self-published his *Life's Little Instruction Book*. Soon thereafter, the book was bought by Rutledge Hill, a local publisher, who went on to sell more than 5 million copies. The book made the bestseller lists in both hardcover and softcover, and continues to be a great seller around graduation time each year.

Author of a previous bestseller, *Permission Marketing*, Seth Godin turned down a generous offer from Simon & Schuster and self-published his book *Unleashing the Ideavirus*. First, though, he gave away the book on the Internet, including a "Tell-a-Friend" link. More than 200,000 people downloaded the book from his web site alone; another 300,000 were exposed to his book through other web sites. He then self-published a $40.00 hardcover edition. Within a week, his book was #5 on the Amazon.com Bestseller List. Twenty weeks after writing the book, he had exposed it to more than half a million people and had already begun making a profit on selling the printed book.

English poet Elizabeth Barrett Browning, author of *Sonnets from the Portuguese*, paid for the publication of her first book.

James Redfield sold 80,000 copies of *The Celestine Prophecy* from the trunk of his car. He then sold the reprint rights to Warner Books for $800,000. The book has gone on to sell 5.5 million copies.

American poet Walt Whitman self-published many editions of his collected poems, *Leaves of Grass* (first edition published on July 4, 1855). *Leaves of Grass* continues to sell thousands of copies each year — almost 120 years after his death!

Ken Blanchard and Spencer Johnson originally self-published *The One-Minute Manager* so they could sell the book for $15.00. All of the experts told them that they'd never sell such a short book for such a high price. In a three-month period of time, however, they sold more than 20,000 copies in the San Diego area alone — and then sold the reprint rights. More than 12 million copies have been sold since 1982, in more than 25 languages.

Richard Bolles originally self-published *What Color Is Your Parachute?* More than 10 million copies have been sold so far in 14 languages.

Deepak Chopra vanity-published his first book and then sold the rights to Crown Publishing. The book became the first of many best sellers for him.

Benjamin Franklin, using the pen name of Richard Saunders, self-published his *Poor Richard's Almanack* in 1732 and continued to produce the *Almanack* for another 26 years.

Novelist Willa Cather paid for the publication of her first book. Her novel *One of Ours* won the Pulitzer Prize.

Dave Chilton self-published *The Wealthy Barber* and made it into a #1 bestseller in Canada, with more than a million copies sold. He then went on to sell an additional 2-million-plus copies in the United States via Prima Publishing.

Wade Cook, through his various companies, has self-published many of his best-selling books, including *Stock Market Miracles* and *Wall Street Money Machine* (500,000 copies sold).

Laura Corn self-published *101 Nights of Grrreat Sex* and several other books. She sold 100,000 copies of *237 Intimate Questions Every Woman Should Ask a Man*, from the trunk of her car. Total sales for *101 Nights* was 525,000 copies as of March 1999. Check out her web site at http://www.grrreatsex.com/.

American poet E. E. Cummings self-published *No Thanks*, a volume of poetry financed by his mother. On the half-title page, he listed the 13 publishers that had rejected the book, which became one of his classics.

Norman F. Dacey self-published the bestseller, *How to Avoid Probate.*

L. Ron Hubbard originally self-published his book, *Dianetics*, which founded a new church, Scientology, and has sold more than 20 million copies over the past 45 years

Sandra Haldeman Martz self-published *When I Am An Old Woman, I Shall Wear Purple*, which went on to sell more than 4 million copies. Prior to this, she had been told that short story collections and poetry do not sell, especially if written by unknown authors.

Richard Nixon self-published one of his books, *Real Peace*.

Tim O'Reilly, President of O'Reilly & Associates, started out as a self-publisher of books about UNIX. He now runs the fourth largest trade computer book publisher, which grew out of his self-publishing efforts.

Your Name Goes Here — with Your Title Here. Let's Get Started Now!

*This list is the result of many hours of research on the Internet. Some of the data were found at www.bookmarket.com, owned by John Kremer.

Appendix

❧ A ☙

The Template

Beginning on a right-hand, odd-numbered page just as it will fall in your book, is a Template that should help you "see" where sections of the book are located and what they will look like, when completed.

While we recommend Times New Roman font in our Template, please note that you can use any standard font in your book.

You may also obtain a Microsoft Word version of this Template on our website at www.bookstandpublishing.com. You can take your manuscript and cut and paste it into this template.

This page was intentionally left blank for the Template to start on the correct page

BOOK TITLE

(Times New Roman 26 pt. and left justified)

For demonstration purposes this template has its own numbering system.

Insert page break here.

(You can use other fonts and similar sizes. Just remember to be consistent.)

Back of "Book Title Page." This page should be BLANK.

Insert page break here.

BOOK TITLE

(26 pt. and centered)

BOOK SUBTITLE (delete if not using)

(14 pt. and centered)

AUTHOR NAME

(12 pt. bold and centered)

Bookstand Publishing
http://www.bookstandpublishing.com

We suggest you insert your web page address here under
Bookstand Publishing.

(10 pt. bold and centered)

Insert page break here.

Published by
Bookstand Publishing
Morgan Hill, CA

ISBN 1-58909-xxx-x
Your ISBN will go above.

Printed in the United States of America

(All text on this page is 10 pt. and centered.)

Insert page break here.

PREFACE (delete if not using)
(12 pt. bold and centered)

The pages before CHAPTER ONE are numbered with Roman Numerals as below. This would be page "v" (five).

If you do not have a Preface, Acknowledgements, or Introduction, the use of Roman Numerals is not needed.

Insert page break here.

ACKNOWLEDGEMENTS (delete if not using)
(12 pt. bold and centered)

SAMPLE TEXT BELOW
To my wife and family for their patience and support;
my longtime friends and new friends discovered during the writing
and publishing of this work.

To the many talented un-published authors waiting patiently to be
discovered.

(All text on this page is 10 pt. and centered.)

Insert page break here.

INTRODUCTION (delete if not using)
(12 pt. bold and centered)

Insert page break here.

A blank page may have to be inserted here to make the Table of Contents start on a right-hand page.

Table of Contents

(16 pt bold and centered)
(If used, it should be a right-hand page unless your Table of Contents requires the use of two pages. In that case it should start on a left hand page.)

The actual table listings should be 10 pt. and left-justified.
Use TABS not SPACES to place page numbers in the table.

Etc.

Insert page break here.

Insert page break here to create a blank page if needed to make the first chapter start on an ODD-numbered, right-hand facing page.

1

(20 pt. bold and centered)

CHAPTER ONE TITLE
(12 pt. bold and centered)
Chapter One Sub-Title (delete if not using)

Chapters should start on an ODD-numbered, right-hand page.
This is only a recommendation. The final decision is yours.

**Always use page breaks between chapters. The excessive use of carriage
returns will cause problems.**

Insert page break here to create a blank page if needed to make the next chapter start on an ODD-numbered, right-hand facing page.

2

(20 pt. bold and centered)

CHAPTER TWO TITLE

(12 pt. bold and centered)
Chapter Two Sub-Title (delete if not using)

ABOUT THE AUTHOR

(10 pt. bold and centered)

About the Author should be on a left-facing page after the last page of text in 10 pt.

One last comment:

You should read and reread your book until you are 100% sure that everything is correct. Once you have done your read-through, give your book to a friend to read, and see whether your friend finds any mistakes.

So many times we are sure that a book is ready to go and we proceed with the printing, only to have an error pop out in the final printed book. One saving grace is that with print-on demand-technology and doing short runs, we have not made a big mistake, only a small one that can be fixed at minimal cost and with little embarrassment.

**Print-on-Demand Publishing
Since 1996**

Are You Ready to Publish Your Book?

Make it Happen!

Contact Us Today — We Can Help!

1-866-793-9365